THEATRES &
OPERA HOUSES

MASTERPIECES OF ARCHITECTURE

TERRI HARDIN

TODTRI

This book was designed and produced by
TODTRI Book Publishers
P.O. Box 572, New York, NY 10116-0572
FAX: (212) 695-6984
e-mail: info@todtri.com

Printed and bound in Singapore

ISBN 1-57717-145-4

Author: Terri Hardin

Publisher: Robert M. Tod
Senior Editor: Edward Douglas
Picture Researcher: Robin Raffer
Designer: Mark Weinberg
Typesetting: Command-O Design

Visit us on the web!
www.todtri.com

PICTURE CREDITS

Photographer/page number

Academy of Music, Philadelphia
Ed Wheeler 51 (bottom)

Bayreuther Festspiele
Jörg Schulze 48, 49

Bayerische Staatsoper
Wilfried Hösl 30 (left)

Culver Pictures 4, 7, 13 (bottom), 28 (bottom), 33 (top),
35 (top & bottom), 50, 53, 61 (bottom)

Deutsche Staatsoper
Marion Schöne 16, 17

Drottningholm Theatre 26, 27

FPG International
Jerry Driendl 62, 68
C. M. Sutton 69
Telegraph Colour Library 40–41
Toyohiro Yamada 45 (top), 46

Glyndebourne Festival Opera 74 (top & bottom)

Grand Opera House, Wilmington 51 (top), 59

Grand Théâtre du Genève 75

Guthrie Theatre
Michael Daniel 77 (bottom)

John F. Kennedy Center for the Performing Arts 66 (top)
Carol Pratt 67

Winnie Klotz 72–73

Maryinsky Theatre
Valentin Baronovsky 39 (top)
Natasha Razina 39 (bottom)

Patti McConville/Les Sumner 65 (top & bottom)

Randall Michelson 58, 70 (top & bottom), 79

Pantages Theatre
Diane Lally 61 (top)

Performing Arts Library, London
Clive Barda 18 (bottom), 33 (bottom), 34, 38, 42 (top), 43

Photo Researchers, Inc.
Herve Donnazan 32
John Farnham 66 (bottom)
Spencer Grant 60
Bobbie Kingley 12
Bob Krueger 52
Frank Maroon 64
Will & Deni McIntyre 54
Bob Moss 57–57
Winston H. Sutter 14

Picture Perfect
Charles Bowman 77 (top)
E, Simanon 28 (top)
Adina Tovy, 11

Santa Fe Opera
Robert Reck 76

SuperStock 5, 10 (bottom), 13 (top), 15, 19 (top), 22, 23, 24–25,
29, 30, 31, 36, 37, 42 (bottom), 44, 45 (bottom), 47, 55, 71, 78

Teatro Communale, Bologna 18 (top), 19 (bottom)

Teatro di San Carlo
Luciano Romano 20, 21

Rudi Von Briel 63

Woodfin Camp & Associates
Robert Frerck 10 (top)
Adam Woolfitt 6, 8–9

CONTENTS

INTRODUCTION

"All the world's a stage," declares an actor to his fellows, as they sit in their makeshift Forest of Arden on a warm summer's day. He continues, "and all the men and women merely players: They have their exits and their entrances. . . ," perhaps making, for all we know, a sly gesture to each side of the stage.

A certain creation of Shakespeare's spoke these words, in 1600, standing on the stage of the Globe Theatre, which the company's protector, the Lord Chamberlain, had had built for them the year before. Common people were crowded into the pit nearest the stage, while aristocrats, royals, and their hangers–on watched the performance from upstairs galleries and a special box known as "my lord's room." The scene was probably boisterous: it was a hot day in August, and everyone who was there was expecting to have a good time.

Four hundred years later, we who attend performances of all kinds have the same expectation, as we give the usher our tickets and are waved to our seats. We sit, and for the most part, we face an upraised platform, framed by an arch, eagerly awaiting the curtain to rise. Perhaps we are even anticipating a performance of *As You Like It*, as did that audience at the Globe so long ago.

The Globe

Not much is known about the architecture of the first Globe, which lasted until June 29, 1613, when—during a particularly exciting performance of *Henry VIII*—a stage cannon, fired to add excitement to the play, set fire to the structure and literally brought the house down. Instead, more is known about the second Globe, which was

ABOVE: This historical drawing of Shakespeare's Globe Theatre gives, if not a detailed, but at least a rough view of the buildings configuration. Elizabethan theatres were always topped by a flag-pole upon which flags were flown to announce the start of a performance.

OPPOSITE: A view of the elaborate decoration of the stage area of the reconstructed Globe.

While no records remain of the interior of the original Globe, it is believed that care was taken with the decoration of the playing area to enhance the spectacle for the audience.

immediately built upon the site of the first. As was the first, this theatre was a circular structure, about 100 feet (30 meters) in diameter, with a yard about 70 feet (21.34 meters) wide. It had three galleries that were 15 feet (4.72 meters) wide, with an overall height of 36 feet (11.13 meters). The stage was nearly 50 feet (15.24 meters) wide and raised above the ground by 6 1/2 feet (2 meters); the ceiling of the stage building met the upper gallery floor at about 60 feet (18 meters), and the *frons scenae* doors were (10 feet (3.35 meters) high.

And this stage—this "world"—how much has the theatre changed after all this time? Would we be comfortable in Shakespeare's Globe? Yes, and no. We would certainly be familiar with its seating arrangement: a circle, interrupted by the stage and its apparatus. (Some people would have better seats, but that's nothing new.) Comfort? Not likely, since it was more or less open to the elements. If we were among the "groundlings" standing in the pit in bad weather, we'd be rained on. Those in the galleries would fare better, but they would still be witnessing a bedraggled spectacle—actors valiantly putting on a play in a thunderstorm.

And we would recognize the Globe's structural arrangement, as would the audiences of ancient Greece, where it all began. They would have been familiar with the amphitheatre—since they had invented it—but they may have eschewed the orchestra level as a place for audience members to stand, since to them this was a part of the staging area. They might have approved the covered balconies, because their theatres were all in the open air, but they might have also felt closed in, since their theatres were also generally much larger.

Greek Beginnings

The theatrical experience, the dichotomy of tragedy and comedy, was also created in ancient Greece. Tragedy is derived from *trogos dios* ("goat song") and alludes to the goat god, Dionysus, god of the vine, for whom festivals were held;

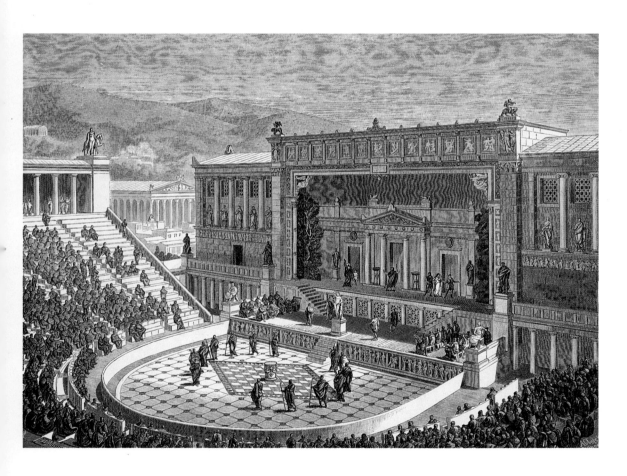

LEFT: This imaginative realization of the Theatre of Dionysus in Athens provides a glimpse of theatres of the ancient world. The audience sat in a raised, semicircular area to observe the play performed on the ground–level *orchestra* or on the main stage, or *skene*, framed by the *proskene*.

FOLLOWING PAGE: Today's Globe Theatre is as close as can be to the original. All classes attended Elizabethan plays with the less fortunate, or "groundlings," standing in the orchestra while the better–off patrons sat in balconies encircling the stage. Here is a modern view of Shakespeare's famous "wooden O."

LEFT: This model, prepared for the reconstruction of the Globe Theatre in London, clearly shows the main elements of the Elizabethan theatre. The building is circular with tiers of balconies for seating, an orchestra area for standees and a covered stage to protect the performers in case of rain. Necessarily, the structure was not roofed over completely, providing ample light for the interior.

ABOVE: Ancient Greek theatres were built into hillsides, providing a natural amphitheatre with astonishingly fine acoustics. Even from this perch at the top, every word could be heard from the stage far below. Unlike today, performances began at sunrise to take advantage of the morning coolness.

ABOVE: One of the main summer attractions in Italy today is a series of opera performances presented in Verona's Roman amphitheatre. Spectacular productions, such as Puccini's *Turandot*, seen here, are staged at one end of the arena, while a vast audience fills the rest of the structure.

and comedy, (*comos dios* or "revel song") was initially a clowning dance; it was also part of the celebrations.

In the beginning, the festival was held in any open, level area, such as the marketplace (*agora*) or threshing floor, which would become, for the purposes of the festival, a dancing floor (*orchestra*). A line of singers (*chorus*) would intone a dithyramb, which would be followed by frenzied dancing, all to the appreciation of an audience. sitting on wooden benches nearby. Several plays were held in competition and judged. Of the many playwrights, three tragedians are famous today: Aeschylus (525–456 B.C.), Sophocles (496–406 B.C.) and Euripides (c.480–406 B.C.); as well as Aristophanes (c.448–c.388 B.C.) the comic playwright.

They were preceded by an innovator. About 534 B.C., a solitary figure appeared against the chorus, addressing them through a linen mask. This innovator was the legendary—and very first—actor, Thespis. Aeschylus, the first great tragedian, introduced the second actor; Phrynichus (c. 512–c.476 B.C.), a tragedian lost to modernity but admired by Socrates, is credited with having introduced the first female character; and Sophocles introduced the third—and last—actor to the play. There might have been more than three characters in the play, but three actors would portray them all, changing masks for different characters.

Elements of Greek Theatres

Dramatic inventions such as multiple characters required staging. In addition to his contribution to the play's cast, Aeschylus is also credited with creating the first *skene*, or scenery. The structure before this was the *proskene*, known today as the proscenium.

At some point, probably having to do with the popularity of the festival, the theatrical milieu was moved to a hillside—a naturally occurring amphitheatre— where benches for more people could be set against the natural incline.

RIGHT: This ancient theatre in Athens is still used for performances. It dates from the Roman period of occupation, when the Romans adopted much that was of value from Greek culture, including its theatrical traditions.

ABOVE: The Roman Colosseum—actually named the Flavian Amphitheatre—had little to do with the arts but much to do with lavish spectacle and cruel and bloody contests. This view from one of the top seats shows the labyrinth of rooms beneath the arena floor that housed gladiators and other performers.

This seating arrangement was called the *cavea* or *theatron*. Below, a flattened *orchestra* space needed to be created. This was achieved by building a retaining wall somewhat farther down the hill, and then filling the space between with dirt. Nearest to the orchestra, on its edge, stood the seats of the dignitaries—priests, rulers, and other notables. This was called the *prohedria*. And since these were religious festivals, an permanent altar and/or temple to Dionysus was placed nearby.

As it happens, still more people were coming to be entertained, and the theatrical setting was again driven to adapt by the demand for spectacle. Dating from the late fourth century B.C., the seating of the theatre began to be built out from the hill, adding more seats and giving greater control to the incline of the arrangement. The important personages who had rated the *prohedria* were further differentiated by having their own circle, still in front.

Thus, as there became more demand for plays, there began to be more permanence to the theatrical structure. Of the ancient theatres, the examples of the Acropolis in Athens and the theatre at Thorikos are most cited, since they are relatively intact. A stone step structure (called the *analemma*) in the shape of a semi–circle took the place of the *cavea*, leading down to the orchestra. At the theatre of Thorikos, the *analemma* had entrances at the back on either side.

Still another example is the Theatre of the Asklepieion at Epidaurus. Attributed to Polykleitos the Younger (c.350 B.C.), who was also the architect of the Tholos at Epidauros, this theatre was considered the epitome of theatrical construction in its own day. To give some idea of the popularity of contemporaneous entertainment, the Asklepieion held more than 12,000 seats, which was not considered unusual.

The theatre at Epidauros was built in two stages, first at the end of the fourth century B.C., when the orchestra, the lower *diazoma* (section) and the stage–building were created; then, about 150 B.C., when the cavea was built up to become 190 feet (58 meters) in diameter (the orchestra was 65 feet (20 metres)., and the *skene* (stage) began to look "modern."

The raised stage (*logeion*) had begun to be part of the theatre accoutrements. Stages were not uncommon but were traditionally the gear of the itinerant comic players (called *phlyaxes*).

LEFT: This 19th–century view of the Colosseum in Rome is a romantic view of a structure that has stood for over two thousand years. Seating up to 45,000 spectators, it was a venue for spectacles from its opening in A.D. 80 until A.D. 404.

BELOW: Following and expanding the Greek model, the Romans built theatres and amphitheatres throughout their empire, both as public amenities and as a way of providing the populace with "bread and circuses." This amphitheatre in Verona, Italy dates from the first century A.D.

Also, by the time of the Epidaurus' second construction, in the second century B.C., the Romans were dominant throughout the world. While they adapted Greek theatres for their own uses (staged naval battles—with a parapet built around the orchestra to form a dam—were popular), they were also capable of building their own. Examples of these are the theatre of Pompeii (55 B.C.) and the Colosseum (A.D. 70–82), both in Rome; and the amphitheatre of Verona. Hadrian's Summertime Theatre (A.D. 125–135) in Tivoli, with its "moat" surrounding a central structure, gives a fair example of a prospective "naval" setting.

The rise of Christianity spelled the demise, for a while, of the theatre and its spectacles. This dark age of theatre began about A.D. 500 and lasted approximately three hundred years. The ban was lifted, curiously, by the church itself, which began to hold pageants and "miracle" (or "moral" plays), to better illuminate the mysteries of Easter. Also, about the mid–sixteenth century, roving troupes of comic actors, known as *commedia dell arte* players had come into demand.

From its triumphant return through religious mysteries, the tide toward theatre as secular entertainment was rising again. And suddenly as well, there appeared a new form of entertainment, called "opera," for which veritable palaces would soon be built.

CHAPTER ONE

SOMETHING FOR EVERYONE

At about the same time that audiences were first watching *As You Like It*, the first opera, *Euridice*, was written by Jacopo Peri in 1600. As was seen in the Introduction, theatre owed much to the religious mysteries, pagan and Christian, as well as to the independent, secular humor that runs through time. The roots of opera were based on a desire to recreate the style of presentation found in ancient Greek drama, which included singing, dancing, instrumental music, and declamation.

To nurture these and other forms of entertainment, forms of architecture evolved, enhancing the theatrical experience for one and all. At first, theatres and opera houses—like all great edifices of the time—were the perquisite of the ruling class who subsidized them; gradually, however, they became available to all classes.

Teatro Olimpico

As was customary with most architecture, some of the first theatre architects looked to their forebears in antiquity. The Teatro Olimpico (1585) in Vicenza, Italy, for example, was based on Roman prototypes from Vitruvius (c.90–c.20 B.C.), whose writing on architecture *De Architecture* (or, more commonly, the Ten Books) had been rediscovered in the fifteenth century and were the basis of Italian Renaissance architecture. The Olimpico's design originated with Andrea Palladio (1508–1580), who was one of the most successful architects of his time, best known for his palaces and villas. Palladio died before the completion of Olimpico, which was undertaken by Vincenzo Scamozzi (1552–1616), who also created the theatre's elaborate trompe l'oeil stage sets that dissolve back into the horizon.

The auditorium of the Olimpico was elliptical instead of the more traditional classical semicircle, allowing it to accommodate more seats (496). Its walls were originally decorated by Francesco Maffei (1600–1660) with narrative friezes and trompe l'oeil effects. In 1750, Cassetti reinforced the Olimpico's classical look by embellishing the structure with a balustrade for a line of statuary behind its tiered

RIGHT: Performances of the past might surprise today's audiences. Not only would acting and performing styles be more broad and histrionic, but the physical setting would seem strange.
Lacking electricity, the stage would be less brightly and subtly lit, the house lights would remain on all night, and audience members would visit and talk—often loudly— throughout.

LEFT: The auditorium of today's La Scala looks much as it did throughout the theatre's history. However, a 1943 bombing attack during World War II destroyed the fabled interior and its stage. The Milanese quickly rebuilt their theatre, and it reopened, completely restored, in 1946.

FRIDERICVS REX APOLLINI ET MVSIS

ABOVE: The Deutsche Staatsoper stands on Berlin's famed Unter den Linden. Originally founded as a court opera by King Frederick II of Prussia in 1741, it has had a notable history as both a musical and ceremonial venue.

rows, and decorating the stage wall in the style of a Roman triumphal arch.

The Olimpico's elliptical design had extended its auditorium to include more seating in a narrower space; however, those who had the side seats, unfortunately, were not able to view the stage, as the proscenium was in the way. In 1628, the horseshoe auditorium, which became standard in theatre architecture, was introduced by Giovanni Battista (Argenta) Aleotti (1546–1636), who created such an auditorium at Teatro

Farnese, a theatre that held 4,500. In the same theatre, Aleotti had created the first proscenium arch ten years earlier, effectively separating the audience from the stage. Both of these were important innovations that would become the norm in modern theatres.

The Court Theatre

While the Olimpico had been built for the Vicenza Accademia Olimpica, a municipal group, often it was royalty that controlled the commissions. The early eighteenth century saw many such theatres, an example of which is the Deutsches Staatsoper (1742) in Berlin.

Like many European buildings, Deutsches Staatsoper has had a long, continuous history, with several incidents of destruction. The renovated structure that was completed in 1955 (based on the original plans but also preserving

expansions following 1844) is the building that is seen today. Originally it was called the Hofoper, and began as a court opera designed by Georg Wenzeslaus von Knobelsdorf (1699–1753) in 1741 for King Frederick II of Prussia. The Staatsoper began its second incarnation on December 7th, 1742. It had the by–now popular horseshoe–shaped auditorium and a seating capacity for 1,396. There were orchestra stalls and three balconies.

The two Langhanses, elder and younger, were involved in important improvements to the Staatsoper. In 1788, Carl Gotthard Langhans the elder (1732–1808), who also designed Berlin's Brandenburg Gate (1788–1791) enlarged its galleries. In 1844, Carl Ferdinand Langhans the younger (1782–1869) reconstructed the theatre (which had been destroyed by fire the year before) and extended the structure on either side to allow room for staircases. Langhans the younger also made

ABOVE: Twice bombed during World War II, today's restored Deutsche Opera in Berlin is a masterpiece of classical restraint. The rebuilding of the theatre, which took about a decade, involved not only modernization but restoration of some of its orginal eighteenth–century design elements.

modifications, raising the roof, adding a fourth balcony, and taking out the ground floor boxes.

Further expansions into this century increased the Hofoper's overall stage capacity, including side and back stages. In 1919, it became the Staatsoper, or State Opera. Its most notorious remodeling to date occurred in 1935, when Paul Baumgarten (1900–1984) was commissioned by the Nazi Party to redecorate the vestibule and foyer in a manner becoming to the Third Reich. These have since been removed.

BELOW: The stage of Bologna's Teatro Comunale has long offered works by the greatest composers, beginning with Gluck's *Il Trionfo di Clelia* in 1763. The theatre is best known for championing the works of Richard Wagner, a composer seemingly at odds with the Italian bel canto tradition.

Italian Theatres

The Teatro Comunale di Bologna (1763) was designed by Antonio Galli–Bibiena, who was a member of a famous family of architects. His bell–shaped auditorium has a capacity of 1,500 seats. Its facade is in the neoclassical style, with two galleries.

Also about this time, one of the most famous of all opera houses, Teatro alla Scala (1778), or more simply, La Scala, was built in Milan. Designed by Giuseppe Piermarini (1734–1808) in the neoclassical style, La Scala has a horseshoe auditorium, with four tiers with separate loges, and two open galleries above. Below, eighteen rows of seats were railed off from the orchestra. (It now has capacity for 2, 200 people in 678 orchestra seats, 409 seats in the first and second galleries, and 155 boxes on four levels.)

One of the ingenious aspects of La Scala is the concave channel under the wooden floor of the orchestra, which is credited with giving the theatre its superb acoustics. This chamber has often been imitated, sometimes, as was the case of the old Metropolitan Opera House in New York, to good effect.

RIGHT: Milan's Teatro alla Scala, or simply La Scala, is perhaps the world's most famous opera house, and the one most closely connected with the development of the art form. Built in 1778, it is associated with the works of such Italian masters as Rossini, Bellini, Donizetti, and Verdi.

ABOVE: Beginning with the simple Renaissance ideal of restoring the drama of the classical world, opera presentations rapidly became more and more sumptuous. Baroque opera was famous for its lavish spectacle, as seen in this view of a musical fete given by Cardinal de la Rochefoucauld at the Teatro Argentina in Rome, July 15, 1747.

LEFT: The Teatro Comunale in Bologna dates from 1763. It was designed by noted architect Antonio Galli–Bibiena, who designed a "bell–plan" auditorium containing four tiers of boxes and a top gallery.

ABOVE: Unlike many other opera houses, the Teatro di San Carlo in Naples
has survived almost intact since its reconstruction after a disastrous fire in 1816.
The magnificent red and gold interior, seen here, dates from 1854.

ABOVE: Early in the nineteenth century the San Carlo was the largest theatre in the world and the most prestigious in Italy. It was the scene of many triumphs for composer Giaochino Rossini whose most popular operas had their premiere on this stage. The importance of the theatre was superseded later in the century by La Scala.

RIGHT: The interior of the Opéra Royal at Versailles appears to be made entirely of marble. However, it is constructed of wood painted to resemble stone. Shown here are the elliptical auditorium, seating a little over 700, and the rather deep stage upon which an original 18th–century stage setting can be seen.

LEFT: The king's box in the Opéra Royal at Versailles. The theatre was built in 1769 by Ange–Jacques Gabriel in preparation for the marriage of the dauphin, the future King Louis XVI, to Marie Antoinette. After the French Revolution, the theatre was used sporadically for various events. Today, special gala performances are given there.

Three French Theatres

Other theatres that originated with royalty were those found at Versailles. The Opéra Royal (1770) and the Théâtre de la Reine originated with the whims of the aristocracy (although one was admittedly more whimsical than the other). The Opéra Royal, which was inaugurated in 1770, was designed by Ange–Jacques Gabriel (1698–1782) who was the principal architect to Louis XV. Gabriel based his design on an existing structure that had been designed by François Mansart (1598–1666). Its interior was faux marble painted on wood. When erected, Opéra Royal was the largest theatre in France, with a capacity of 712.

The Théâtre de la Reine was built at the Petit Trianon by architect Richard Mique at the behest of Marie Antoinette. Marie Antoinette gave several performances, along with her "Company of Nobles." Although the theatre was opulently furnished and provided with "state–of–the–art" stage machinery by Bouillet, its seating was modest.

The Bourbons had scant time to enjoy these theatres. The Opéra Royal was closed by the French Revolution, but reopened under Louis–Philippe in 1837. From 1876 to 1879, it was also used by the senate of the Third Republic, who made the theatre its seat, and rebuilt the stage and reinforced the overall structure to ensure its suitability. From 1952 to 1957, it underwent a major restoration.

Another victim of the Revolution to stand the test of time was the Grand–Théâtre (1780) of Bordeaux. Styled a "cathedral theatre" (theatres basilisques) on account of its reverentially conservative design and mass. The Grand–Théâtre was designed by Parisian architect Victor Louis (1773–1780) by commission from the Marechal Duc de Richelieu.

The Grand–Théâtre was the first to have colonnades along its public areas. With this theatre, the roof of the auditorium and elevated stage tower are visible above the balustrade. The roof was made of wood and the columns of the portico were reinforced with iron. Its auditorium originally contained 1,158 seats.

This impressive theatre has as much public space as it does auditorium and stage spaces. In 1837, the space above the vestibule to the 700–seat concert hall was transformed into a ballroom and then into a foyer. In 1853, restorations were made to its interior. Both reconstructions were supervised by Charles–Bernard Burguet. In 1915, machinery was installed that raised the orchestra stalls to be level with the stage.

FOLLOWING PAGE: Intermission at a French theatre of the 19th century. Meeting friends, seeing and being seen, and wearing one's finest clothes were important aspects of theatre–going. Not only was conversation constant, but in some theatres, wealthy patrons would give supper parties in their boxes, adding the clink of glass and silverware to the sounds from the stage.

Successive restorations have been lavished on the Grand–Théâtre, the latest by Bernard Fanquernie in 1991, which saw the renovations of reception rooms, auditorium, and stage apparatus. The Grand–Theatre now seats 1,114 in its bell–shaped auditorium, with four levels of balconies.

The Grand–Théâtre was damaged during the French Revolution but restored in 1799 in the First Empire style. In 1871, the Third Republic was proclaimed from the theatre, and it became the seat of Parliament during the siege of Paris.

From Sweden to Bavaria and Russia

Like Marie Antoinette, Sweden's Queen Louisa Ulrike was also fond of theatre and desired one of her own, to be built at her residence in Drottningholm. Unlike the French queen, she preferred to watch performances from a well–placed royal box. Designed by Carl Frederick Adelkrantz in 1764, Drottningholm's auditorium seats a modest 454. In 1791, a foyer for entertaining was created by Jean–Louis Desprez.

Karl von Fischer designed the Bayerische Staatsoper (1818) for Maximilian I, king of Bavaria. Neoclassical in design, it had a portico capped by a triangular pediment, which was over a second tympanum that filled the gable of the roof's ridge. It was linked to the Court Theatre (1753) by a covered passage.

Now known as the Cuvilliés Theatre, it was designed by François Cuvilliés the elder, a court dwarf in the service of Maximilian. Its many distinctions include having had the

ABOVE: The theatre at Drottningholm Palace, just outside of Stockholm, is a perfectly preserved 18th–century theatre, complete with stage machinery of the period and original scenery for thirty productions. After being forgotten for over 100 years, it was rediscovered in 1921 and has been devoted to special presentations ever since.

RIGHT: The auditorium of Drottningholm Theatre, originally a court theatre, features different kinds of seating: large throne–like chairs for royalty and other exhalted persons, plain benches for court members, and lattice–enclosed boxes for nobles who wished to see performances without being seen themselves.

ABOVE: One of Russia's premier theatres, the Bolshoi in Moscow has survived fire, war, and revolution. Its splendid neo-classical portico, topped by a statute of Apollo in his chariot, is a precursor to the splendors of the magnificent gold and red auditorium to be found within.

RIGHT: The Gran Teatro La Fenice in Venice is one of Italy's most illustrious theatres. Aptly named, The Phoenix, it has risen from its ashes several times since its opening in 1792. Regrettably, this magnificent building was again consumed by flames in 1996 and is being rebuilt.

world premieres of two Mozart operas (*La Finta Giardiniera*, 1775, and *Idomeneo*, 1781).

When the Staatsoper was destroyed by fire in 1823, the neoclassical architect Leo von Klenze (1784–1864) reconstructed it, and introduced a second, polychromatic pediment above the portico. The reconstructed theatre was opened in 1825.

In 1943, the Staatsoper was destroyed by bombing. In 1963 the restored building reopened; the reconstruction followed the original plan, with the grand staircase and foyer restored to the 1825 version.

Moscow's Bolshoi Theatre (1825) was constructed on the site of the Petrovsky Theatre, which dated from 1780 until it was destroyed by fire. The Bolshoi (or "big theatre") was constructed by Ossip Bove with Andrei Mikhailov.

Boasting an Ionic facade, the interior of the Bolshoi features a horseshoe auditorium with a capacity of 2,150 seats; these are to be found in four balconies and a top gallery. It has excellent acoustics.

The Bolshoi is well known not only for opera but for its celebrated ballet company (originally begun in 1773 as a dancing school for orphans). In 1918, Moscow was restored as the capital of Russia, and the Bolshoi regained preeminence over the Maryinsky Theatre (1860) in St. Petersburg, to which it had been unfavorably compared (much as is Moscow with that fair city).

The Danger of Fire

The vicissitudes of war are one thing, but if there is one single fate that lays low theatres and opera houses alike, it is fire. Whether or not they had stone exteriors, inside, they were a fantasy of wood, plaster, and fine cloth; luminously lit by hundreds (if not thousands) of candles, crowded with spectators, most of them milling and jostling each other for a better view. In short, before electricity, theatres were little better than tinderboxes, waiting for that unlucky strike.

One theatre made a virtue of its fiery fate. The legendary Gran Teatro La Fenice (the "phoenix") in Venice was built in 1792, upon the site of the former Teatro San Benederro, which had been destroyed by fire in 1774. A competition was held for its design, and was won by Gianantonio Selva.

La Fenice was the first neoclassical building in Venice. It faced a plaza, and in the back, had its own canal, dug to provide access to the backstage area. La Fenice had a seating capacity of 1,500 and was built in a horseshoe shape, with three tiers of

LEFT: A performance at the Comédie Française in the late 18th century. The company was established by Louis XIV in 1680 and has been devoted from that time until today to presenting the great classics of French drama. Its home theatre was destroyed by fire around 1900, but was rebuilt soon after.

boxes and two galleries. Its gilded decor was overlaid with blue. It originally had had 70 boxes, which were identical and rose in tiers around the horseshoe. An "imperial box" was created in 1808, in honor of Napoleon Bonaparte (1769–1821). The auditorium was also redecorated by Guiseppe Borsato.

When the theatre was again destroyed by fire in 1836, it was rebuilt by Tommaso and Giambattista Meduna, based on Selva's original design and opened the next year. Then, a trompe l'oeil pergola was painted by Transquillo Orsi, and the hall was decorated in Empire style by Sebastiano Santi.

During the revolutions of 1848, the imperial box was briefly destroyed, but was later restored and redecorated by Meduna and Borsato. In 1854, the theatre was redecorated by the brothers Meduna in the Rococo style. In 1937, La Fenice became the property of the city of Venice and a modern stage and machinery was installed; Nino Barbarini restored the decor. Even so,

ABOVE: The auditorium of today's National Theatre, or Bavarian State Opera, in Munich is a modern version of the early 19th–century neoclassical designs created for the original theatre. Severe wartime bomb damage necessitated the complete rebuilding of the structure.

about fifteen years later, Vera Stravinsky, attending the premiere of her husband's work, *The Rake's Progress* in 1951, noted that the "plush [of the stalls] seems to have had chicken—or rather, moth—pox, and it seems everything else is badly in need of deodorants. Another discomfort is that the seats are like European railroad compartments. The occupants on the side nearer the stage (i.e., the men) face in the wrong direction as if their ears were encased in their legs and abdomens, like grasshoppers."

LEFT: This painting by Adam Heinrich shows the appearance of Munich's National Theatre in the mid–19th century. It was built close to the royal palace and was connected to the much smaller court theatre by a covered walkway.

In 1996, another fire broke out, destroying La Fenice. However, the "phoenix" is expected to rise again with a program of restoration to the original Selva design and Meduna decoration by the millennium.

Theatres in Changing Times

Noblesse oblige required the aristocracy to share its good fortune in public works. Thus, although built by royalty, people of all walks of life could enjoy themselves at such court-sponsored theatres as the Bayerische Staatsoper in Munich and the Theater an der Wien in Vienna. The Bolshoi, once an aristocratic enclave, was opened to the general public in 1880 at the order of Tsar Alexander III.

However, the true age of the public theatre would arrive as royalty lost its hold on the populace, and the colonies of the New World beckoned with untold wealth that anyone (or so it was believed) could claim. A new kind of bourgeoisie would arise to spend it.

CHAPTER TWO

COMING OF AGE

The nineteenth century saw opera raised to a high and popular art. Not only did lyric theatres proliferate throughout Europe, but the newly discovered or acquired territories were clamoring for this fashionable and glamorous art form as well. These included Africa, the Near East and South America; as well as North America, with its upstart cities of the Far West.

By this time as well, the trend toward commission by competition, rather than princely appointment, was becoming entrenched. This meritocracy, for the most part, pitted the best against the best, or at least allowed a fresh perspective to emerge more frequently than before.

A Royal Theatre

Of the opera houses built in this time, the Royal Opera House at Covent Garden (1858) is among the most renowned. The Theatre Royal (1732) was the first playhouse built on its site. This structure was designed by Edward Shepherd and financed by famous impresario John Rich on the proceeds of his *Beggar's Opera* (1728).

ABOVE: There has been a London theatre known as Drury Lane, or Theatre Royal, since 1663. The site of many outstanding theatrical events, this view of the theatre dates from c. 1750. The building shown here was designed by Christopher Wren in 1674 and stood until it was destroyed by fire in 1791.

LEFT: Barcelona's Gran Teatro del Liceu is one of the glories of Spain and is the pride of the Catalan region which it serves. Built in 1861, it was the site of many great musical performances, especially those featuring Spain's finest artists and singers. It was destroyed by fire in 1994, and is currently in the process of being completely restored.

LEFT: The auditorium of London's Royal Opera House is much admired for its intimacy and for its stately decoration, complete with deep red curtains and royal insignia. It served as a model for American planners, who incorporated many of the theatre's elements into the construction of New York's Metropolitan Opera in 1883.

The first musical star of Covent Garden was Georg Friedrich Handel (1685–1759) who wrote operas and oratorios expressly for the theatre, including the premiere of *Messiah* (1743). Upon his death, he bequeathed to Rich his organ, which a fire destroyed—along with the theatre—in 1808. Another theatre was built a year later.

In 1847, the Covent Garden auditorium was completely remodeled to the designs by Benedetto Albano, and the theatre began its brief incarnation as the Royal Italian Opera, featuring the works of such favorites as Gioacchino Rossini (1792–1868). In fact, at the theatre's inauguration, Rossini's *Semiramide* was performed.

The present Covent Garden dates from 1858, built after another fire destroyed the Royal Italian Opera House in 1856. It is for this theatre that E.M. Barry designed a new horseshoe auditorium supported by a metal framework, thus eliminating the standard support columns for tiers and balconies and improving sight lines.

ABOVE: The Royal Opera House, Covent Garden as it appears today. The glassed–in area under the portico was created in 1899 to add a bar and to increase public space for the audience. Though, unlike other opera houses, it escaped wartime damage, it was closed during World War II and used as a dance hall for the armed forces.

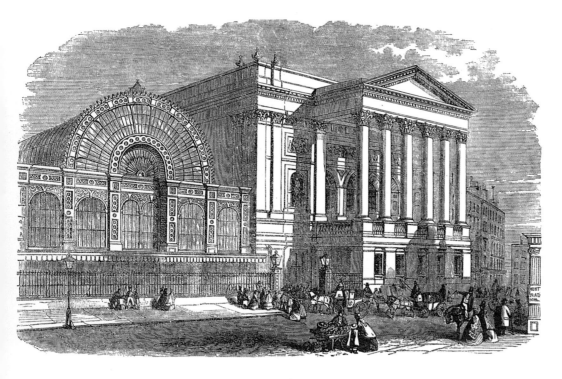

LEFT: Today's Royal Opera House, Covent Garden opened in 1858. Four years later, the owners built an addition, known as Floral Hall. Intended for use as a flower-selling space by day and as a concert hall in the evening, the building had little success. Not surprisingly for a structure made of glass and iron, the hall's acoustics were poor, and it was soon turned into a warehouse.

ABOVE: The direct precursor of today's Royal Opera House, Covent Garden was the Royal Italian Opera, seen here as in appeared in 1822. The theatre fell victim to fire in 1856. London had long been consumed by a vogue for opera ever since Handel's day in the 18th century. This theatre catered to an interest in the then fashionable Italian bel canto repertory.

ABOVE: More than any other music–loving Europeans, the English were captivated by
the oratorio, a form developed and popularized by Handel, involving a dramatic
situation or theme that was sung with orchestral acommpaniment, but not staged or acted
out. This oratorio performance at Covent Garden in 1800 is typical of the period.

ABOVE: The Theatre Royal, Drury Lane, has long been at the
center of London theatrical life and has seen many outstanding
performers and productions. This view is typical of the often
spectacular fare offered at the theatre in the late–18th century.

Fit For a Tsar

Other theatres have led similar, checkered lives. The Circus Theatre, devoted to Russian opera, was built in St. Petersburg in 1855 but burnt down in 1859. This theatre was then reconstructed by Alberto Cavos, becoming the Maryinsky Theatre in 1860.

After the Russian Revolution, the Maryinsky was known from 1919 to 1935 as the National Academy Theatre of Opera

BELOW: This view of the auditorium of the Maryinsky Theatre in St. Petersburg shows the results that involved royal patronage has produced. Built in 1860, as the home of the imperial opera and ballet companies, as well as a social setting for the court of the tsars, this regal interior has seen many outstanding productions, particularly in the realm of ballet.

and Ballet. It was then renamed a second time to honor Sergei Kirov, a prominent Soviet politician of the period. The theatre was evacuated during the second world war, rehabilitated in 1963, and became the Maryinsky once again in 1990 soon after the dissolution of the Soviet Union.

The Maryinsky has a horseshoe auditorium and seating capacity for 1,621. Although it was designed primarily for opera, the Maryinsky has generally been known for its association with ballet. The apex of its fame came when it was home to the Imperial Ballet Company and the great Tchaikovsky ballets were created and first produced. Many legendary names of ballet—including Diaghilev, Nijinsky, and Pavlova—are associated with the Maryinsky, as are those of more modern recognition such as Nureyev, Makarova, Baryshnikov, and Balanchine.

FOLLOWING PAGE: It is fitting that a city so renowned for its architectural jewels and devotion to the arts as Dresden should have an opera house as fine as the one designed and built by Gottfried Semper in 1878. Though completely destroyed in World War II, it was carefully and magnificently reconstructed according to Semper's designs, reopening in 1985.

LEFT: The imperial box, located in the center of the Maryinsky's tier of boxes, was reserved strictly for the use of the tsar and his family, who regularly appeared for premieres and gala evenings. The box, standing two tiers high, was topped by a representation of the Russian crown. Removed during the Russian Revolution, it has recently been restored.

BELOW: The exterior of the sprawling Maryinsky Theatre in St. Petersburg is similar to some of the other monumental buildings in this city. The use of pastel color with white trim brings brightness to a sometimes gray northern climate. Fortunately, the theatre was spared damage during the 900–day Siege of Leningrad by Nazi forces in World War II.

The Vienna Staatsoper

In 1860, as part of a citywide renewal, the Emperor Franz Joseph of Austria–Hungary (1830–1916) held a competition for the design for a new opera house which would be known as the Hofoper, or Court Opera. The commission was won by Eduard van der Null and August Siccard von Siccardsburg. The new theatre was completed in 1869 and inaugurated with a performance of Mozart's *Don Giovanni*.

The design for the theatre was influenced by the Italian Renaissance style, and contains a grand staircase and a horse-shoe auditorium with four tiers of boxes. However, the auditorium today, with its capacity of 2,276 seats, is quite different from the original one. Late in World War II, the opera house was severely damage by bombs which gutted both the auditorium and stage area. Remarkably, the foyer, grand staircase, and other public areas remained unharmed. When the restored opera house reopened in 1955, the public discovered that the design of the new areas was much simpler and more restrained, and lacked many of the nineteenth–century flourishes of the old auditorium.

Known today as the Staatsoper, or State Opera, the theatre is the center of Vienna's thriving musical life and a symbol of Austrian national pride.

ABOVE: The restored auditorium of the Vienna State Opera was first seen in 1955 when the theatre re-opened soon after the Russian occupation of Austria ended. The apt choice for the reopening was Beethoven's *Fidelio*, a hymn to freedom and liberation.

LEFT: Opened in 1869 as the Vienna Court Opera, or Hofoper, the theatre is most widely known today as the Staatsoper (Vienna State Opera). Its reputation as the center of Viennese musical life has long been established, and it remains as one of the world's great opera houses.

RIGHT: The grand staircase of the Vienna State Opera gives an idea of how the entire theatre looked when it was new. Though the exterior of the building was severely criticized, the splendid interiors met with great success. The staircase and other public areas escaped destruction from a 1943 Allied air raid, while the auditorium and stage house did not.

The Palais Garnier

The Paris Opera is among the few theatres that have survived intact. Officially called the Palais Garnier–Opéra National de Paris (1875), this famous theatre began when, in 1861, Charles Garnier (1861–1874) won its commission over such competitors as Eugène Emmanuel Viollet–le–Duc (1814–1879). Construction, however, took fifteen years and was interrupted by the Paris Commune of 1871 when it was briefly turned into a prison during the siege of Paris.

Those familiar with the Paris Opera note its opulent decor, almost unchanged but for the 1962 Marc Chagall ceiling fresco that obscures the original Jules–Eugene Lenepveu painting without destroying it. Chagall painted his new work on panels that were placed over the original fresco so that it could be preserved.

Aside from building a suitable theatre for opera and ballet, perhaps Garnier's greatest contribution is the creation of the rich and striking interiors that so successfully capture the tastes and attitudes of Second Empire France. These are some of the greatest ceremonial spaces in the world and provide a sense of occasion to any event.

ABOVE: In 1962, famed Russian artist Marc Chagall was asked by then Minister of Culture, Andre Malraux, to prepare new frescoes for the center of the Palais Garnier's ceiling. The brightly colored results adds a fresh modern touch to the theatre without conflicting with the formal character of the interior.

RIGHT: Spectacular and ethereal scenic effects have long been achieved through the use of rope and rough wooden wheels and gears. This ancient machinery beneath the stage of the Palais Garnier has been augmented by more modern equipment.

LEFT: The main façade of the Palais Garnier, or Opéra National de Paris, is an imposing sight in a city filled with architectural marvels. The richly ornamented classical front is surmounted by an immense dome. Massive statuary groupings on the top of the roof and on either side of the dome complete the monumental effect.

ABOVE: There is no public space in the world that can match the splendor of the grand staircase of the Palais Garnier. Conceived as a glamorous meeting place for the elite of Napoleon the Third's Second Empire, the staircase, as does the rest of the building, epitomizes the aspirations and longing for grandeur found in mid–19th century France.

RIGHT: This view of the Palais Garnier's auditorium, as seen from the stage, shows the striking contrast between the theatre's richly styled public spaces and the more mundane, workaday backstage area. In 1995, all the stage machinery was updated to incorporate the latest technological advances.

A Wagnerian Triumph

Of theatres associated with composers, there is perhaps none like the Festspielhaus (1876) in Bayreuth, which had a composer as one of its primary architects. Richard Wagner, with the help of Otto Bruckwald and Karl Brandt, and with the backing of King Ludwig II of Bavaria, built this theatre according to his own specifications.

Specifically designed for the presentation of Wagner's operas, the 1,925–seat theatre has a fan–shaped auditorium, with boxes lining the rear wall and a balcony above the entrance (added in 1882). The Festspielhaus has a double proscenium arch and a deep, spacious orchestra pit with room for a 130–member orchestra, the sight of which is obscured from the audience's view. Audience members are not distracted by the movement of performing musicians or the glare of lights from music stands. Instead, they see only the action on stage accompanied by a wave of sound from the orchestra that fills the acoustically perfect hall. The wedge–shape of the auditorium draws the eye irresistibly to the stage and contributes greatly to the exceptional quality of the sound. The theatre was Wagner's dream, and it remains under the control of his heirs to this day.

LEFT: The Festspielhaus in Bayreuth, Germany was designed solely for the presentation of the works of Richard Wagner. The theatre built for the first performances of Wagner's four–opera cycle *The Ring of the Nibelung*, was actually intended to be only temporary. A more imposing and innovative building was planned, but never built due to lack of funds.

ABOVE: The interior of Wagner's Festspielhaus was unique for its day. The orchestra seating was wedge–shaped, allowing for better sight lines and superb acoustics. Side boxes were banished, and only a single row of boxes was built across the back of the auditorium.

Opera Comes to the New World

Meanwhile, the Europeans who were pouring into the New World were bringing with them their passion for opera. In the colonies, opera performances had been enjoyed as early as 1702. From the first, the opera and its houses were *de rigueur* in the New World's oldest cities; George Washington attended an opera in New York City during the first year of his presidency.

The first great performance centers for opera, however, began to appear in the mid–nineteenth century. One of the earliest notable theatres was the Academy of Music (1857) in Philadelphia. It was designed by the Philadelphia building partnership of Napoleon Le Brun and Gustavius Runge, who nevertheless had to win a national competition in 1852 in order to build it.

The Academy mostly mimicked La Scala's semi–circular tiers of seats, curving around an almost cylindrical area. Its upper tiers are reinforced by Corinthian columns made from cast–iron, which give the impression of private boxes while being open on the sides. (This actually improves the sightlines in the upper tiers.) Below, the Academy's private boxes are stacked on each side of the stage, and kneeling statues support the auditorium's ceiling. Its chandelier hangs in the midst of a fresco that is attributed to Constantin Keiser; other ceiling murals portraying the arts are by Karl Heinrich Schmolze. Unlike many of its peers in the New World, the Academy has been changed little since its inception, having always been treasured by its city.

A new fashion, cast ironwork that could be bolted and soldered together, created the main facade of the Grand Opera House (1871) of Wilmington, Delaware. (In this case designed by Royce Brothers Company of Philadelphia, cast ironwork was the "pre–fab" rage of the day, an entire buildings–worth could be ordered from a catalog and delivered ready–to–build to any site.) The Grand Opera House's ironwork was then painted with a faux chiseled–marble scheme.

Restored by the Victorian Society of America in 1971, this theatre nonetheless differed from others in that it was originally designed by architect Thomas Dixson as a Masonic temple in French Second Empire style. It seems reminiscent of the theatre at Bordeaux. Its exterior was made up of three tiers of columns below a mansard roof. Inside, instead of a main chandelier, the opera house had smaller light fixtures at the ceiling corners.

LEFT: Philadelphia's Academy of Music, opened in 1857, is America's oldest opera house still used for its original purpose. The exterior was deliberately designed to be as plain as possible, so that more money could be spent to make the interior appropriately sumptuous. Succeeding generations have not regretted this decision.

LEFT: One of the most encouraging trends of the last quarter century has been the inclination to repair and restore old buildings instead of destroying and replacing them with modern buildings of dubious esthetic value. Here, the carefully restored interior of Wilmington's Grand Opera is seen.

LEFT: The proscenium and stage as seen from the top balcony of the Academy of Music in Philadelphia, Pennsylvania. The Philadelphia Orchestra, seen here in rehearsal, is the owner of the theatre and shares it with various local opera, ballet, and concert groups.

The American Midwest

Sometimes described as "Sauerbraten Byzantine," the Cincinnati Music Hall (1878) was composed of four million bricks, and erected for the city's May festival in 1878. Its exterior was a mass of polychromatic brick and stone, and it had a rose window in its center.

BELOW: The Wheeler Opera House, built in Aspen Colorado in 1889 is typical of theatres built in the 19th–century American West. Cities and towns of any pretension—and some had quite a lot—boasted at least one theatre of medium size that was grandly called an opera house. Some, such as the Wheeler shown here, have survived and been lovingly restored.

Designed by Cincinnati architects Hannaford & Proctor, the Music Hall combined three buildings under one roof. The northern wing was originally used as a sporting arena (it is now used as a rehearsal hall and for scenery storage), and the southern section was used up to 1967 as an exhibition center. In the center, the Springer Auditorium—named after its chief sponsor, Reuben Springer—can seat 3,600. In 1895, the auditorium's gallery and proscenium arch were added. It has been a National Historic Landmark since 1975.

Most opera houses have stories surrounding their building, and New York City's first Metropolitan Opera (1883) is no exception. Built by "parvenus" as a slap in the face to old New York Society (who had given them the cold shoulder), the Met

LEFT: The original Metropolitan Opera House (1883) was built by a group of newly rich New Yorkers who wanted a large theatre with an adequate number of private boxes to satisfy their artistic and social ambitions. Though the theatre had many flaws, its opulent auditorium was not one of them, giving rise to the name "Diamond Horseshoe" for the tiers of boxes filled with glittering patrons.

competed with, and eventually triumphed, over previous New York institutions such as the Academy of Music and the Astor Place Opera House.

A competition for its design was won by Josiah Cleaveland Cady, who had designed New York's Museum of Natural History, but never an opera house. After winning, however, Cady went on a tour of Europe's great opera houses, admiring La Scala not a little.

New York and Points West

The Metropolitan Opera was designed on an irregular plot of land, which required some modifications of the original design and short–changed the building of necessary backstage storage areas. In front, the Met originally had four rows of boxes, with 12 *baignoire* boxes at the "orchestra circle." Above these were 38 parterre boxes; the "grand tier" and "dress circle" had 36 boxes each.

It was styled "the yellow–brick brewery" by its detractors. Certain aspects were considered risible, such as the fact that some of the uppermost seats had no view of the stage. What could not be diminished, however, was the sound. For peculiar reasons (some thought the egg–shaped acoustical chamber beneath the stage may have been a factor), the auditorium was supposed to have had practically no reverberation. These acoustics and the theatre's sheer size—more than 4,000 seats in a semi circle of boxes—made the Metropolitan unique. It was demolished in 1966 after the Metropolitan Opera Company moved to its new home in Lincoln Center for the Performing Arts.

Throughout the country, palaces of culture were being built. Generally, the towns that raised them were flush with new money, such as the mining town of Aspen, Colorado with its Wheeler Opera House (1889), and the port towns of New Orleans (Old French Opera House, 1859) and Galveston (Grand Opera House, 1894).

Theatres of Latin America

Not to be outdone by the newly wealthy industrials of the United States, the rubber barons of South America were also keen on opera and as keen to show it.

The Teatro Municipal de Santiago (1857) was inaugurated with Verdi's *Ernani*. Originating in 1853 with the Ministry of the Interior under the presidency of Manuel Montt, it was designed (with influences of Charles Garnier) and constructed by architect Francisco Brunet de Baines and engineer Augusto Charme. In 1870, the theatre was partially destroyed by fire, but was reconstructed and reinaugurated three years later.

The Teatro Colón in Buenos Aires was completed and opened in 1908. The first-night audience was no doubt happy to attend, since the theatre had been under construction for twenty years under the direction of several architects. These included Francesco Tamburini, Vittorio Meano, and Jules Dormal. Given the number of people involved in its construction and planning, it is not surprising that the building runs the gamut of styles associated with European theatres. In 1925 it became the municipal theatre of Buenos Aires.

Under construction for fifteen years, the Teatro Amazonas (1896), or Amazon Theatre, in Manaus, Brazil, is a tribute to the wealth and perseverance of the rubber barons of that time. The theatre was a complete European import, for even if some of the materials used in its making came from nearby, they were sent to Europe to be "fashioned," as the barons no doubt sent their daughters to European finishing schools, whenever possible.

The theatre is topped by a dome in which a mosaic was created using 36,000 vitrified ceramic tiles. The capacity of the auditorium is 700 seats, 250 of which are in the orchestra, and 450 in 90 boxes in three tiers of balconies, as well as a special box reserved for dignitaries. Artists associated with the Amazon Theatre include Brazilian artist Crispim do Amaral, who painted the drop curtain and the Italian, Domenico De Angelis, who decorated the Noble Room.

BELOW: The Palacio de Bellas Artes in Mexico City is one of the most spectacular buildings devoted to the arts in the Americas. Begun in 1905 and because of political and economic difficulties not completed until 1934, it nevertheless proved worth the wait, as this aerial view clearly shows. The interior is noted for its Art Deco motifs.

Like others in the New World, Palacio de Bellas Artes (1934) represented the tendency in the New World to look toward Europe for inspiration. Begun in 1904, and designed by Italian architect Adamo Boari (1863–1928), the Palacio was organized around a great hall, with a funnel–shaped triple cupola between the lobby and the theater.

LEFT: When wealthy planters decided to build an opera house in Manaus, Brazil, in the heart of the Amazon, they spared no expense of detail and construction. The result was the Teatro Amazonas (1896) which thrived until a severe depression ended regular performances in 1907. In 1990, the theatre was completely restored and now presents a range of cultural events each year.

FOLLOWING PAGE: The interior and exterior magnificence of the Teatro Colon in Buenos Aires (1908) is matched only by its outstanding record of high artistic achievement. Practically all of the world's greatest singers and conductors have appeared here in a wide array of productions.

Completion of the Palacio was interrupted by various types of unrest, which included earthquakes and the Revolution of 1910. In 1916, Boari left the country, and it was not until 1932, when the Mexican architect Federico Marshal (1881–1971), undertook its direction. Marshal was influenced by the European style, Art Deco, but also incorporated pre–Columbian ornaments such as the Mayan eagle, the Mayan water gods Tláloc and Chaac, as well as other deities. Other Mexican luminaries who have decorated the Palacio include Diego Rivera, Jose Clemente Orozco, David Alfaro Siqueiros, and Rufino Tamayo.

Theatres and Show Business

But while the high art of opera was concerning the high–minded, the light entertainments—popular song and dance, magic tricks and sleights of hand, circus acts, jokesters, and "guest lectures"—were also commanding a wide, if not wider audience. In the mid–1800s, to accommodate this rage, entrepreneurs in England had begun to build large–scale performance, or music, halls that offered a wide variety of entertainments for a small amount of money.

Modest as their clientele was, the takings were good, and the music halls began to imitate the opera houses in a plethora of styles. Among the primary architects was Frank Matcham (1854–1920), who, in 1901, opened the Hackney Empire and the Coliseum (1904) in London.

The Hackney Empire had seating for 2,000 and was completely electric (the first of its kind in Great Britain) and

had a projector box for moving pictures—the shape of things to come. Design was a feverish combination of Moorish, Gothic, and Rococo. The Coliseum was faux Roman and even larger.

Across the Atlantic, light entertainment was traveling under the name of vaudeville. At first, its entertainers gave performances wherever they could—small theatres, music halls, and saloons. As in England, theatres dedicated to vaudeville were springing up across the face of America. These included the Orpheum Theatre (1921) in Minneapolis and the Oriental Theatre (1926) in Chicago. Other, older theatres were refitted as vaudeville theatres, then as movie houses. Such was the fate of Wilmington, Delaware's Grand Opera. In 1921, an electric marquee affixed to its entrance proclaimed it simply, "Grand."

Going to the Movies

Out of the vaudeville theatres were born the movie palaces, although—from the nickelodeons to the silents through to talking pictures—vaudeville did coexist, sharing the stage with the new entertainments. And nowhere else were these theatres more elaborate than in Hollywood. Grauman's Chinese Theatre (1927), the Egyptian (1922), and the Pantages in Los Angeles are legends among the movie palaces.

Designed by the architectural firm of Meyer and Holler (who appeared to make a specialty of temple fantasies), the 2,200–seat Chinese and the 1,800–seat Egyptian represented the exotic experience of seeing a film. Even today, watching

LEFT: The recently restored Egyptian Theatre in Los Angeles gives modern multiplex–patrons, a view of what the total movie–going experience was like to audiences earlier in this century. The exuberant interiors of theatres such as these enhanced fantasies of all kinds created by the Hollywood dream machine. The deep orchestra pit recalls the era when silent films were accompanied by full orchestra in the larger theatres.

RIGHT: With the advent of such popular entertainment forms as vaudeville and motion pictures, many theatres formerly devoted solely to theatrical productions were converted to new uses. This is what happened to the stately Grand Opera in Wilmington, Delaware which was turned into a movie house and renamed the Grand.

a film in what is now Mann's Chinese Theatre is a singular experience.

So, too, is that experience in New York City's Radio City Music Hall (1932). Designed by Donald Deskey, Radio City is an Art Deco behemoth, almost a cathedral to pop culture that seats up to 5,000 people.

Radio City's stage measures 65 feet (20.26 meters) in depth and is an amazing 145 feet (43.89 meters) wide. It also has four hydraulic elevators, which can descend 25 feet (8.23 meters) into the basement or rise 15 feet (3.96 meters) above the stage. The elevator system can move an entire orchestra to the front or the back of the stage during performances.

LEFT: One of the most famous of the old movie palaces is the Pantages Theatre in Los Angeles. It is also known for being the home of many stage productions. This view of the auditorium reveals a house less extravagant than most of its type, but rich in detail, as demonstrated by the intricate geometric design of the coffered ceiling.

RIGHT: Radio City Music Hall, opened to the public in 1932, is one of the main attractions of Manhattan's Rockefeller Center. Seating 5,000 and equipped with stage elevators, a revolving stage, and even the ability to produce a shower of rain, the stage shows presented here have never been less than spectacular. This vintage photograph captures a revue from the 1940s.

LEFT: The exterior of Mann's Chinese Theatre in Los Angeles still conveys the same Hollywood magic that it had when previously named Graumann's Chinese Theatre. Renowned for its exotic interior, this building from 1927 is also noted for its famous sidewalks, bearing the signatures and footprints of legendary movie stars.

Radio City retains its original 1932 Wurlitzer organ, which has a separate console on each side of the stage. One may imagine its awe–inspiring proscenium to be an imitation of a Wurlitzer jukebox; however, it is supposed to be a recreation of a sunset as seen from aboard a cruise ship.

San Francisco

As the twentieth century advanced, the popular entertainment industry grew rapidly. However, the lust for opera houses, while no longer at its zenith, had not waned completely. San Francisco's War Memorial Opera House (1932) is a prime example. Considered one of the best houses in the New World,

it was designed by Arthur Brown, Jr. who also designed San Francisco's Coit Tower and City Hall. The theatre has a capacity of up to 3,252 seats, although two rows are generally removed during the opera season to accommodate the orchestra, bringing capacity down to 3,176.

In 1989, the Loma Prieta earthquake damaged the War Memorial Opera House, and it was closed for a year and a half while renovations amounting to $84.5 million were undertaken. In the past, as was done before, people might have considered razing the house and building a new one; however, as the twentieth century comes to an end, we have begun to hold onto our cultural past, even as we look ahead to the future.

ABOVE: The War Memorial Opera House in San Francisco, designed by Arthur Brown and opened in 1932, has been a force in turning the city into one of the major arts centers in the United States. In addition to its cultural legacy, it is noted for being host to the signing of the United Nation's Charter in 1945.

RIGHT: From its beginning, the regular daily fare of New York's Radio City Music Hall was a feature–length motion picture followed by a one–hour stage show, featuring variety acts that included the world–famous Rockettes. Today, though movies are no longer presented, spectacular productions, such as the annual Christmas show, regularly sell out the hall.

CHAPTER THREE

ALWAYS AND FOREVER

Though the character of the arts and entertainment has changed radically during the past one hundred years due to developments in technology, the value of theatres remains undiminished. In fact, the place of performance is more important to us than ever, for not only has performance architecture actually reached a scale previously unheard of, but efforts are being made around the world to cherish the theatres that have come down to us through the ages.

Arts Centers

Of the large–scale arts venues, three of the most significant in the latter half of the twentieth century have been New York City's Lincoln Center (1966), the John F. Kennedy Center for the Performing Arts (1971) in Washington D.C., and the Sydney Opera House (1974) in Australia.

Lincoln Center was conceived as an urban renewal project for a notorious tenement neighborhood on Manhattan's upper west side. Just before it was demolished and replaced with the present cultural mecca, the neighborhood enjoyed one last hurrah as the location for the film, *West Side Story*. Lincoln Center houses most of the city's major cultural institutions, including the Metropolitan Opera, the New City Opera, the New York Philharmonic, and the New York City Ballet, all of which were moved from disparate performance spaces throughout the city. The architects for this noble institution are among the greatest names of the day, including Wallace Harrison, who designed the Metropolitan Opera House; Philip Johnson, architect of the New York State

ABOVE: The centerpiece of Lincoln Center is the Metropolitan Opera House—the "new" Met—designed by Wallace Harrison. It's bright, open exterior is in sharp contrast to its predecessor, which presented a grim, gray façade to the street. At night, the theatre is ablaze with light, inviting passersby to come in and enjoy the evening's musical offering.

ABOVE: The New York State Theatre (1964), in New York's Lincoln Center for the Performing Arts, was designed by then–modernist architect Philip Johnson. Collaborating with George Balanchine, artistic director of the New York City Ballet, Johnson originally planned a theatre devoted solely to dance. It has since been modified to accommodate opera and other forms.

LEFT: A bust of President John F. Kennedy is prominently placed in the lobby of the Kennedy Center. The commitment to the arts of the president and his wife Jacqueline, as well as a wish to honor the slain leader's memory, was an important factor in gaining the approval and funding needed to complete this project.

ABOVE: Long considered only a political town, the arts have thrived in Washington since the opening of the Kennedy Center in 1971. The Center includes an opera house (shown here), a concert hall, the medium–sized Eisenhower Theatre, and two smaller theatres designed for experimental productions.

RIGHT: The Barbican Centre in London is a vital addition to an already thriving musical and dramatic scene. Opened in 1982, it is the London home of the Royal Shakespeare Company, the London Symphony Orchestra, and the Guildhall School of Music and Drama.

Theatre; and Max Abramowitz who was responsible for Avery Fisher Hall.

The focal point of Lincoln Center is the new Metropolitan Opera House. A picture of gilded modernism, the new Met embraces the horseshoe auditorium style with seating for 3,824 in orchestra and four balconies, along with one tier of boxes and four tiers of side boxes. It has about 800 more seats than did the old Met, the "yellow brick brewery" that was torn down, in spite of its handsome interior, to make way for a more efficient and up–to–date performing space. The new opera house also offers larger public areas than the old one did. A sweeping grand staircase, a spacious restaurant, and a sumptuous promenade area on the grand tier level of the house are a few of the amenities now available to audiences.

Five years after Lincoln Center was inaugurated, the John F. Kennedy Center for the Performing Arts opened in Washington, D.C. Designed by Edward Durrell Stone, the center includes a 2,350–seat opera house, a 2,750–seat concert

ABOVE: The John F. Kennedy Center for the Performing Arts in Washington, D.C. fulfills a long–standing need in the nation's capital. For years, there was no suitable theatre for presenting large–scale productions or for staging the type of ceremonial and diplomatic events expected by visiting heads of state and other dignitaries.

hall, and the 1,100–seat Eisenhower Theater, all of which are accessed by a grand foyer. Two smaller performance spaces, the 500–seat Terrace Theatre and the 400–Seat Theatre Lab, are on the second, or Terrace, level.

Most theatres are devoted to art, but the Kennedy Center has an additional ceremonial purpose: it serves as the official venue of the nation's capital. As such, the center also features a Hall of Flags, honoring nations with whom the United States maintains friendly status. Many of these nations also contributed building materials and decor as part of their diplomatic mission.

The most significant achievement of the century in performance architecture, however, must be the Sydney Opera House. Viewing it from the air as one flies into the city, one sees a phenomenal structure that dwarfs all other buildings.

The redoubtable Opera House is really a complete performing arts center, containing various venues such as a 1,547–seat opera theatre, a 2,690–seat concert hall, a 544–seat drama theatre, and a 398–seat playhouse, which is also used as a cinema. Interiors are paneled in wood for acoustical as well as aesthetic reasons. The major performance spaces have their own foyers, whose enormous glass windows look out into Sydney Harbor.

The opera house stands on a point in Sydney Harbor, support-ed by 580 concrete piers sunk up to 80 feet (25 meters) below sea level. It was nearly fifteen years in the making. The primary concept belongs to Danish architect Jorn Utzon, who won the international competition for its design in 1957. The now–famous shell design of its roof vaults was originally thought impossible, and had to be redesigned by the architect. The vaults were then cast into 2,194 concrete sections, weighing about 15.5 tons each, assembled with tensioned steel cable, and covered with over one million tiles. The roof is supported by 32 concrete columns that are about 8 feet– (2.5 meters–) square. Glass, another significant material to the building's design, was fitted into the mouths of the roof shells, as well as throughout the building.

ABOVE: Though the Sydney Opera House, magnificently sited on land jutting into Sydney harbor, has become a symbol of Australia recognized around the world, there are significant design flaws. Because of its unusual and provocative silhouette, the theatre devoted to opera production lacks many elements essential to the production of opera on a grand scale.

RIGHT: The lobby of the Sydney Opera House offers spectacular view of Sydney harbor as well as spacious areas for audiences visiting the center's many performing venues.

RIGHT: This view of the façade of the Alex Theatre in Glendale, California shows the value of retaining architecture from the past. Buildings like these, with their playful exuberance—although not comparable to Frank Lloyd Wright or Mies van der Rohe— nevertheless add color and excitement to our movie– and theatre– going experiences.

RIGHT: Egyptian, Asian, and Moorish motifs were favorites of both architects and movie audiences. Though not precisely accurate in their details and styling, compared to authentic examples, they still provided a basic visual education to a public not exposed television, video, the Internet, and the barrage of images available today.

An Interest in the Past

And what of the other theatres, from ancient to modern? What is being done with them? Blessedly, they are being restored in record numbers; and many are again in use.

There's the realization of how the delights of an earlier age can appeal to the modern one, such as the recent restoration of E. M. Barry's cast iron Floral Hall at Covent Garden. (Cast iron, the building material of the Victorian age, is enjoying a renaissance.) Then there's the restoration of old vaudeville and movie houses, such as the aforementioned Egyptian in Los Angeles (now a museum and performance center); and the Fox Theatre (1929) in Atlanta, Georgia. Designed by Mayre, Alger and Vinour, this restored jewel of a movie house is breaking its long string of bad luck that began with the ruination of its original owners in the Depression. It is now a film and performance theatre.

LEFT: The Fox Theatre in Atlanta, Georgia is an outstanding landmark. Designed for movies and stage shows, it has a large stage and orchestra pit. The performing spaces are so ample that the theatre was home for many years to the Metropolitan Opera when it visited the city on tour.

FOLLOWING PAGE: Here is a view of an opening night audience at the Metropolitan Opera with artistic director James Levine on the podium. Opened in 1966, the house has many improvements over the "old Met," not the least of which is a reconfigured seating plan that offers good visibility to at least 95 percent of the audience.

RIGHT: For many people, attendance at the Glyndebourne Festival Opera requires a train or motor trip from London into the English countryside. There, on the Christie family's estate, a modern theatre offers the finest opera productions, and the spacious grounds are an ideal pastoral setting to enjoy strolling or picnic suppers during the long intermissions.

ABOVE: In contrast to the original 400–seat theatre built at Glyndebourne in the 1930s, the new auditorium will accommodate 1,200 comfortably. Improved stage equipment also ensures lively and creative productions. Originally specializing in the works of Mozart, the Festival now explores an eclectic range of composers and periods.

And there's the high tech edge. Following the 1989 Loma Prieta earthquake, San Francisco's War Memorial Opera House underwent a transformation, not only to make it as earthquake–proof as possible, but to outfit the theatre with advanced technology while maintaining the acoustics for which the theatre had become famous. To this end, everything in the theatre—fixtures, seats, etc,—was subjected to new up–to–date tests to see what effect they would have on the acoustics. Finally, it was given a state–of–the–art sound system.

Like the War Memorial Opera House, the Glyndebourne Opera House (1994), originally a small country theatre of 300 seats, has elevated science for the service of art with proper acoustics determined by computer simulation. Designed by Michael Hopkins the new Glyndebourne Theatre now has a capacity of 1,200 seats, in orchestra, two balconies, and a gallery. The Glyndebourne's *modern* interior contrasts interestingly with its Victorian, red–brick exterior.

RIGHT: When it comes to rebuilding damaged theatres, their are two choices: an exact, detailed replication of the original or an updated version, adapting old designs to contemporary styles. In restoring the fire–damaged Grand Théâtre de Genève, planners chose the latter option as shown in this view of today's interior

In spite of all the technological advances in theatrical acoustics, many attend the arts of opera and drama in contemporaneous or even classic settings, because doing so adds to the overall experience. For example, to attend a performance at Radio City Music Mall, with a pageant, the Rockettes, and picture feature, might bring on a pleasant bout of nostalgia. Many go to the theatres of the Bolshoi, the Paris

ABOVE: New Mexico's Santa Fe Opera is one of America's most appealing summer attractions. Designed originally as an open air theatre, it is now completely roofed over, affording audiences cooling summer breezes and views of the spectacular Western landscape, while protecting them from the often unpredictable elements.

LEFT: Opened in 1986, the Musiektheater in Amsterdam is one of the world's newest opera houses. Its fan-shaped auditorium seats 1,600 people in an orchestra section and two balconies. The up-to-date and spacious backstage area make quick, smooth scene changes possible.

BELOW: The Tyrone Guthrie Theatre in Minneapolis, Wisconsin was opened in the late 1950s. Its main features are an audience seating area that almost surrounds the performers and a thrust–stage that brings the drama closer to viewers. It was thought that this type of plan would replace rectangular, proscenium theatres, but this prediction has proved false.

Opera, and La Scala not only to enjoy a performance but to sit in the place of history. Attending the Verona opera festival, where the audience sits in a Roman amphitheatre and experiences acoustics more magically precise than modern science allows, is exalting.

Interestingly, those who seem particularly passionate about viewing their artist *in situ* are devotees of Shakespeare. For this reason, replicas of the Globe Theatre appear throughout the world. The most faithful adaptation can be found in London, with the Shakespeare Globe Playhouse (1994), now part of the International Shakespeare Globe Center at Bankside.

Conceived by American actor Sam Wanamaker and designed by Pentagram Design from archaeological analysis and original documents. The playhouse has been recreated within 600 feet (183 meters) of its original site, with materials that would have been used in its original construction. There are about 900 seats and 700 standing places.

Thus, we find people filing into today's Globe as eagerly as they must have done four hundred years before, awaiting in the open air, come what may, a good show. For us, as it has always been, the theatre building is part of that timeless experience.

ABOVE: One of the success stories of 20th–century opera–building is the Opéra de la Bastille in Paris, opened in 1989. Completely contemporary in every way, it appeals because of its total break with conventional opera house design. Devoted exclusively to opera, it has attracted large and enthusiastic audiences, and has been important in revitalizing the operatic scene in Paris.

RIGHT: The grant of landmark status to certain important buildings and the growing trend in preserving and restoring unique structures from the past has ensured that our architectural heritage will not be destroyed. Shown here is a detail from the refurbished Egyptian Theatre in Los Angeles.

INDEX